I0020795

INVISIBLE EYES:

UNDERSTANDING AI MONITORING AND THE FUTURE OF OUR PRIVACY

SUBTITLE: DIGITAL PRIVACY REVOLUTION: NAVIGATING AI SURVEILLANCE AND DATA PROTECTION

By Robert Anderson Love Wins

http://RobertAndersonLoveWins.com

TABLE OF CONTENTS

Book Description:..8

    This essential guide covers:..8

    Perfect for readers interested in: 10

Invisible Eyes: Understanding AI Monitoring and the Future of Our Privacy 11

    Digital Privacy Revolution: Navigating AI Surveillance and Data Protection 11

        What You Will Discover: 11

Introduction 13

Chapter 1: What is AI Monitoring? 15

    Definition of AI Monitoring 15

    How It Works 15

    Common Applications 16

    Summary.. 17

Chapter 2: The Data We Generate 19

    Types of Data Collected 19

    Who Collects the Data 20

    The Concept of Data as a Commodity............................ 22

    Summary.. 23

Chapter 3: Implications for Personal Sovereignty 24

    Understanding Personal Sovereignty 24

    Erosion of Autonomy... 24

    Case Studies: Surveillance and Personal Freedoms 25

Summary.. 27

Chapter 4: Security Concerns 28

Data Breaches and Cybersecurity Risks..................... 28

Government Surveillance... 29

Impact on Vulnerable Populations............................. 30

Summary.. 31

Chapter 5: Misuse Possibilities 32

Manipulation and Control 32

Predictive Policing and Bias.. 33

Surveillance Capitalism 34

Summary.. 35

Chapter 6: The Call for Regulation and Transparency ... 37

Current Regulatory Landscape 37

The Need for New Regulations.................................... 38

Best Practices for Transparency 39

Summary.. 40

Chapter 7: Empowering Individuals 42

Educating the Public 42

Tools for Protection... 43

Advocacy and Activism 44

Summary.. 45

Chapter 8: The Future of Privacy and AI 47

Emerging Technologies and Trends............................ 47

Vision for a Privacy-Conscious Society 48

Call to Action 49

Summary 50

iPhone 51

1. Siri and Voice Recognition 51

2. Location Services 51

3. Health and Fitness Monitoring 52

4. System Analytics and Diagnostics 52

5. Personalization and Suggestions 53

6. Data Syncing with iCloud 53

7. Apple's Ecosystem Integration 53

AI monitoring on an iPhone 54

1. Location Tracking 54

2. App Permissions 55

3. Usage Data Collection 55

4. Background App Refresh 56

5. Artificial Intelligence Algorithms 56

6. Third-Party Tracking 56

7. Data Backups 57

Android 58

1. System Services and Features 58

2. Voice Recognition 58

3. System Analytics and Diagnostics 59

4. Personalization and Suggestions 59

5. Data Syncing and Backup 60

6. Device Health and Performance Monitoring 60

7. Device Settings and Permissions 61

AI monitoring on an Android device 62

1. Location Tracking 62

2. Voice Assistants and Recognition 62

3. App Permissions and Background Activity 63

4. Usage Data Collection 63

5. Behavioral Profiling 63

6. Data Syncing and Backup 64

7. Third-Party Tracking and Ads 65

8. Device and Network Monitoring 65

Windows on your PC 67

AI Monitoring on Windows Computers Without User Knowledge 67

1. Windows Services and Features 67

2. Background Applications and Processes 68

3. Internet Browsing and Online Activity 68

4. Microsoft Account Integration 69

5. System Updates and Diagnostics 70

6. Remote Access and Monitoring 70

7. Data Backups and Storage 71

Case Study 1: Cambridge Analytica Scandal 72

Data Harvesting Process 72

Targeted Advertising 73

Ethical and Legal Implications 73

Conclusion 74

Case Study 2: GDPR Implementation 75

Background 75

Key Provisions of GDPR 75

Impact on Businesses 76

Challenges Faced 77

Conclusion 78

Educating the Public on AI Monitoring and Privacy 80

Raising Awareness 80

Empowering Individuals 81

Advocacy for Regulation and Transparency 82

Fostering an Engaged Citizenry 83

Suggested comprehensive regulations for AI data collection and its
use 85

1. Informed Consent Requirements 85

2. Data Minimization Principle 85

3. Right to Access and Portability 86

4. Transparency and Algorithmic Accountability 87

5. Data Breach Notification Requirements 87

6. Establishment of Data Protection Officers (DPOs) 88

7. Privacy by Design and Default 89

8. Regular Audits and Compliance Checks 89

9. User Empowerment and Education Initiatives 90

10. Cross-Border Data Transfer Regulations 90

Combating the overreach of AI data collection on cell phones and systems 92

1. Strengthening Data Protection Regulations 92

2. Enhancing Transparency and Accountability 93

3. Empowering Users 93

4. Supporting Privacy-Centric Alternatives 93

5. Implementing Technological Solutions 94

6. Advocacy and Public Pressure 94

7. Legal Action and Litigation 95

Addressing government overreach in AI tracking and surveillance 96

1. Advocacy for Stronger Data Protection Laws 96

2. Foster Public Awareness and Education 96

3. Encourage Transparency and Accountability 97

4. Engage in Legal Challenges 97

5. Build Alliances and Coalitions 98

6. Promote Alternative Technologies 98

7. Engage in Public Discourse 99

8. Promote International Standards 99

In an increasingly interconnected world, the unseen forces of AI monitoring are reshaping our lives, often without our consent. Invisible Eyes: Understanding AI Monitoring and the Future of Our Privacy is a groundbreaking exploration of how artificial intelligence tracks, analyzes, and influences our personal data, raising critical questions about privacy and autonomy.

THIS ESSENTIAL GUIDE COVERS:

- The Mechanics of AI Monitoring: Uncover the technologies behind AI surveillance, from smartphones to smart home devices. Learn how these systems collect data and the implications for your privacy rights.

- Real-World Case Studies: Dive into compelling case studies, including the infamous Cambridge Analytica scandal and the far-reaching impact of GDPR regulations. Understand the risks of data overreach by corporations and governments.

- Practical Privacy Strategies: Equip yourself with actionable steps to protect your personal information. Discover essential privacy tools, effective consent practices, and strategies for managing your digital footprint.

- Advocacy for Change: Learn how to advocate for stronger data protection regulations and demand transparency from tech giants. Join a growing movement dedicated to fighting against the overreach of surveillance.

- Future-Proofing Your Privacy: Stay informed about emerging privacy technologies and legislation. Gain insights into how to navigate the rapidly evolving digital landscape while safeguarding your rights and freedoms.

Invisible Eyes is a crucial resource for anyone concerned about the implications of AI monitoring on personal privacy. Whether you're a tech enthusiast, a privacy advocate, or simply someone wanting to understand the digital landscape better, this book provides the knowledge and tools you need to reclaim control over your personal data.

Join the digital privacy revolution today! Empower yourself with the insights to thrive in a world where your privacy matters.

PERFECT FOR READERS INTERESTED IN:

- Digital Privacy

- AI Surveillance

- Data Protection

- Privacy Advocacy

- Consumer Rights

- Technology Ethics

In a world dominated by digital technology, our every move is increasingly tracked and analyzed by powerful AI systems—often without our knowledge or consent. Invisible Eyes takes you on an eye-opening journey into the realm of AI monitoring, revealing how these technologies are reshaping our lives, our rights, and our understanding of privacy.

WHAT YOU WILL DISCOVER:

- The Hidden Mechanics: Learn how AI surveillance operates, from the devices in your pocket to the algorithms behind the scenes. Understand the data collection processes that shape your online experience.

- Real-World Impacts: Explore compelling case studies, such as the Cambridge Analytica scandal and the implementation of GDPR, to grasp the true implications of data overreach by governments and corporations.

- Your Privacy Toolkit: Equip yourself with practical strategies to safeguard your personal information. Discover essential tools and techniques to manage your digital footprint effectively.

- Advocacy for Change: Find out how you can become an advocate for stronger data protection laws. Learn how to demand accountability from tech giants and participate in the growing movement for digital rights.

- Navigating the Future: Stay ahead of emerging trends in privacy technology and legislation. Understand how to protect your rights in a rapidly evolving digital landscape.

Invisible Eyes is a vital resource for anyone seeking to navigate the complexities of AI monitoring and understand the future of personal privacy. Whether you're a concerned citizen, a technology enthusiast, or simply looking to protect your data, this book provides the insights you need to reclaim control over your digital life.

Join the digital privacy revolution today!

Book Title: Invisible Eyes: Understanding AI Monitoring and the Future of Our Privacy

Subtitle: Digital Privacy Revolution: Navigating AI Surveillance and Data Protection

INTRODUCTION

Purpose of the Book

- Rationale for Writing: In an era where technology is woven into the fabric of daily life, understanding the implications of AI monitoring on privacy and personal sovereignty is essential. This book aims to illuminate the often-hidden practices of data collection and surveillance, empowering readers with knowledge about their rights and the systems that govern their digital interactions.

- Importance in Today's Digital Age: As smartphones, social media, and connected devices become ubiquitous, the amount of personal data generated is unprecedented. This data can be used for various purposes, from improving services to surveillance and manipulation. The book seeks to raise awareness about these practices and their implications for individual rights, security, and societal structures.

The Digital Landscape

- Technological Integration in Daily Life: Discuss how technology has transformed everyday activities, from communication and shopping to navigation and entertainment. Highlight the reliance on smartphones and the internet in modern life.

- Data Generation: Explain how everyday actions—such as sending a text, sharing a social media post, or using a GPS app—generate vast amounts of data that are collected and analyzed by corporations and governments alike.

- Emerging Technologies: Introduce the role of artificial intelligence in processing and interpreting this data, making it possible to monitor behavior and predict actions on an individual and societal level.

- Overview of the Surveillance Environment: Set the stage for the discussion on AI monitoring by discussing the current state of surveillance in society, including the normalization of data collection and the public's general unawareness of the extent of this monitoring.

By establishing the purpose and context in the introduction, readers will have a clear understanding of why the book is relevant and what they can expect to learn about the implications of AI monitoring on their lives and society as a whole. This foundation will prepare them for the deeper exploration of the topics in subsequent chapters.

DEFINITION OF AI MONITORING

- Understanding AI Monitoring: AI monitoring refers to the systematic collection and analysis of data from individuals using artificial intelligence technologies. This process involves gathering information through various digital devices—such as smartphones, computers, and smart home devices—and employing AI algorithms to interpret and act upon this data.

- Data Collection Methods:

- Passive Data Collection: This includes background data that is collected without user intervention, such as location data from GPS, browsing history from web activity, and app usage statistics.

- Active Data Collection: This involves data that users intentionally provide, such as filling out online forms, participating in surveys, or posting on social media.

- Sensors and IoT Devices: Smart devices equipped with sensors (like smart thermostats, fitness trackers, and smart speakers) continuously collect data on user behavior and preferences.

HOW IT WORKS

- Data Aggregation: AI monitoring begins with the aggregation of vast amounts of data from multiple sources. This data can include user interactions, device sensor readings, and even external data sources (e.g., social media platforms).

- AI Algorithms: Once the data is collected, AI algorithms process it to identify patterns and trends. Key components include:

- Machine Learning: This subset of AI uses statistical techniques to enable computers to learn from data and improve their performance over time without explicit programming. Machine learning models can recognize behaviors, preferences, and anomalies.

- Natural Language Processing (NLP): NLP allows AI systems to understand and interpret human language, which can be used to analyze text from social media posts, emails, and customer reviews.

- Predictive Analytics: By analyzing historical data, AI can make predictions about future behavior, allowing companies and governments to tailor their services or policies accordingly.

- Real-Time Monitoring: Many AI monitoring systems operate in real time, allowing for immediate responses to user behavior, such as targeted advertisements based on recent searches or alerts for location-based services.

COMMON APPLICATIONS

- Social Media Monitoring: Platforms like Facebook and Twitter use AI algorithms to analyze user interactions and behavior, allowing for personalized content delivery and targeted advertising. This includes monitoring likes, shares, comments, and even sentiment analysis of posts.

- Location Tracking: Apps such as Google Maps and delivery services use GPS data to provide navigation assistance and optimize delivery routes. However, this constant tracking raises concerns about user privacy and the potential for misuse of location data.

- Smart Devices: Smart home devices like Amazon Echo and Google Nest collect data on user preferences and habits to offer convenience. For example, smart thermostats learn about your schedule to adjust temperatures automatically, but they also gather data about your daily routines.

- E-commerce and Targeted Advertising: Online retailers use AI to analyze browsing and purchase history, enabling them to recommend products tailored to individual preferences. This targeted advertising is based on extensive data collection and predictive analytics.

- Healthcare Monitoring: Wearable devices, such as fitness trackers and smartwatches, collect health-related data (e.g., heart rate, activity levels) that can be analyzed to provide insights into personal health and fitness, but they may also share this data with health providers or insurance companies.

SUMMARY

In this chapter, we have defined AI monitoring and explored its foundational components, including data collection methods and the workings of AI algorithms. By examining common applications of AI monitoring in everyday life, we highlight how pervasive these technologies have become. Understanding these concepts is essential for grasping the implications of AI monitoring on personal privacy, sovereignty, and society as a whole. The next chapter will delve deeper into the data generated by our digital interactions and the implications of this data collection on our lives.

TYPES OF DATA COLLECTED

In our increasingly digital lives, smartphones and connected devices generate a vast array of data. Understanding the types of data collected is crucial for recognizing the extent of monitoring and its implications for privacy. The following are key categories of data collected from smartphones:

- Location Data: This includes GPS coordinates that track where a user is at any given moment, as well as historical location data, which can reveal patterns of movement over time. Apps such as maps, ride-sharing services, and social media often collect this information to provide personalized services.

- Browsing History: Every website visited, search query made, and link clicked is recorded. This data is used to build user profiles for targeted advertising and content recommendations. Browsers and search engines often store this information, which can include timestamps and interaction details.

- Communication Data: This encompasses text messages, emails, and calls. While some apps offer end-to-end encryption, metadata (such as who communicates with whom and when) can still be collected by service providers and analyzed.

- App Usage Data: Information about how often and for how long users engage with various applications is captured. This data helps companies understand user behavior and preferences, leading to improved product development and targeted marketing.

- Health and Fitness Data: Wearable devices and health apps track metrics such as heart rate, sleep patterns, and physical activity levels. This data is often shared with health providers, insurance companies, or can be sold to third parties for research purposes.

- User Preferences and Interests: Data about users' preferences, including liked content, saved items, and purchase history, is collected by apps and platforms to personalize the user experience and improve engagement.

WHO COLLECTS THE DATA

Various stakeholders are involved in the collection and utilization of personal data. Understanding these key players is essential for recognizing the broader implications of data monitoring:

- Tech Companies: Major technology firms (e.g., Google, Facebook, Apple, Amazon) are primary data collectors. They gather extensive information from users to enhance their services, improve user experience, and drive targeted advertising. Their business models often rely on monetizing user data.

- Advertisers and Marketing Firms: Advertisers use collected data to create targeted marketing strategies. By analyzing user behavior and preferences, they can deliver personalized ads, increasing the likelihood of consumer engagement and sales.

- Government Agencies: Various government bodies may collect data for national security, law enforcement, or public health purposes. This can include monitoring communications, tracking locations, and accessing data held by tech companies, often under legal frameworks or emergency orders.

- Third-Party Data Brokers: These companies aggregate data from various sources, including public records and online activities, to build detailed profiles on individuals. This data is often sold to businesses for marketing purposes, which can further erode personal privacy.

- App Developers: Many applications collect user data to provide features and services. Some may share this data with third parties for marketing or analytics, leading to further dissemination of personal information.

The commodification of personal data has transformed how information is perceived and utilized in the digital age. Understanding this concept is vital for grasping the implications of data collection:

- Monetization of Data: Personal data is increasingly viewed as a valuable asset. Companies collect, analyze, and sell this information to advertisers and marketers, who leverage it to craft targeted campaigns. The more detailed the data, the higher its value, leading to a data-driven economy.

- Implications for Privacy: The commodification of data raises significant privacy concerns. Individuals often lack control over their personal information, which can be shared, sold, or used in ways they may not approve of. This situation can lead to a sense of vulnerability and a feeling that one's privacy is being invaded.

- Ethical Considerations: The practice of treating personal data as a commodity raises ethical questions about consent, ownership, and the right to privacy. Many users are unaware of the extent of data collection and how their information is being used, leading to calls for greater transparency and regulation.

- Data Exploitation Risks: As data becomes a commodity, the potential for exploitation grows. Companies may prioritize profit over user rights, leading to practices such as invasive tracking, manipulation through targeted advertising, and unauthorized data sharing.

SUMMARY

In this chapter, we have explored the various types of data generated through our digital interactions, identified the key players involved in data collection, and examined the implications of treating personal data as a commodity. Understanding these elements is essential for recognizing the privacy risks associated with AI monitoring and the need for regulatory frameworks that protect individual rights. The next chapter will delve into the implications of these data practices on personal sovereignty and security, highlighting the broader societal impacts of AI monitoring.

UNDERSTANDING PERSONAL SOVEREIGNTY

- Definition of Personal Sovereignty: Personal sovereignty refers to the inherent right of individuals to govern themselves, make their own choices, and maintain control over their personal information and privacy. In the context of privacy, personal sovereignty emphasizes the importance of consent and the ability to make informed decisions about how one's data is collected, shared, and used.

- Privacy as a Fundamental Right: Personal sovereignty is closely tied to the concept of privacy, which is recognized as a fundamental human right. The ability to keep certain aspects of one's life private fosters autonomy, freedom of thought, and the capacity to express oneself without fear of judgment or reprisal.

EROSION OF AUTONOMY

- Constant Monitoring and Its Effects: The advent of AI monitoring leads to an environment where individuals are continuously surveilled, often without their explicit consent or knowledge. This constant oversight can create a sense of vulnerability and powerlessness, undermining personal sovereignty.

- Impact on Decision-Making: Knowing that one is being monitored can alter behavior and decision-making processes. Individuals may self-censor their thoughts and actions to conform to perceived societal norms or expectations, limiting their ability to express themselves freely or explore new ideas.

- Freedom of Expression: The fear of being watched can discourage individuals from engaging in open discussions, sharing controversial opinions, or participating in social movements. This chilling effect stifles creativity, innovation, and the diversity of thought necessary for a healthy democratic society.

- Internalized Surveillance: The psychological impact of being monitored can lead to "internalized surveillance," where individuals begin to regulate their own behavior to align with external expectations. This self-censorship can diminish authentic self-expression and inhibit personal growth.

CASE STUDIES: SURVEILLANCE AND PERSONAL FREEDOMS

- Political Dissent: In countries with authoritarian regimes, surveillance technologies are often used to monitor political dissenters and activists. For example, in China, the government employs extensive surveillance systems, including facial recognition and social credit systems, to track and control citizens' behavior. This has resulted in the suppression of free speech, the targeting of activists, and the chilling of political dissent.

- Social Movements: The use of surveillance during social movements can have a profound impact on individual participation. During the Black Lives Matter protests in the U.S., law enforcement agencies employed various surveillance tactics, including monitoring social media and using drones. This level of scrutiny has led some individuals to hesitate in joining protests for fear of retaliation, thereby undermining the collective power of social movements.

- Workplace Surveillance: In many workplaces, employers have implemented monitoring technologies to track employee productivity and behavior. For instance, remote monitoring software can record keystrokes, track online activity, and even capture webcam footage. While intended to increase efficiency, such practices can create a hostile work environment, eroding trust and autonomy among employees. Workers may feel pressured to conform to company expectations, stifling creativity and innovation.

- Data Breaches and Abuse: High-profile data breaches, such as the Cambridge Analytica scandal, illustrate the potential for misuse of personal data. In this case, personal data collected from millions of Facebook users was exploited to influence political campaigns without their consent. This incident highlights how the commodification of personal data can undermine individual sovereignty and manipulate public opinion.

SUMMARY

In this chapter, we have explored the implications of AI monitoring on personal sovereignty, emphasizing the erosion of autonomy and the impact on individual decision-making and freedom of expression. Through real-life case studies, we have illustrated how surveillance can suppress dissent, inhibit participation in social movements, and create environments of self-censorship. Understanding these implications is essential for recognizing the urgent need for regulatory measures that protect individual rights and promote a society that values personal sovereignty. The next chapter will examine the security concerns associated with AI monitoring, focusing on the risks posed by data breaches and misuse of personal information.

DATA BREACHES AND CYBERSECURITY RISKS

- Understanding Data Breaches: A data breach occurs when unauthorized individuals gain access to sensitive or confidential information, often resulting in the exposure of personal data. These breaches can occur due to hacking, human error, or inadequate security measures.

- Cybersecurity Risks: The collection of vast amounts of personal data creates attractive targets for cybercriminals. Common risks associated with data collection include:

- Hacking: Cybercriminals may exploit vulnerabilities in systems to steal large datasets containing personal information. High-profile hacks, such as those affecting Equifax and Yahoo, have exposed millions of individuals' personal information, including Social Security numbers, credit card details, and more.

- Identity Theft: With personal data readily available, identity theft has become a significant concern. Criminals can use stolen information to impersonate individuals, opening fraudulent accounts, making unauthorized purchases, or committing other crimes. This can result in devastating financial and emotional consequences for victims.

- Phishing Attacks: Data collected through monitoring can be used to craft sophisticated phishing schemes, where attackers use personal information to manipulate individuals into providing additional sensitive data or accessing malicious links.

- Long-Term Consequences: The ramifications of data breaches can be long-lasting. Victims of identity theft may spend years recovering their identities, facing challenges in credit applications, employment, and personal relationships.

- Government Access to Data: Governments often access personal data for various purposes, including national security, law enforcement, and public health. While these objectives may be well-intentioned, the implications of such surveillance practices can be concerning.

- Potential for Abuse of Power: The potential for government abuse of power increases with access to personal data. Examples include:

- Overreach and Monitoring: Governments may misuse surveillance technologies to monitor political dissent, gather intelligence on activists, or suppress freedom of speech. This has been observed in countries with authoritarian regimes, where data collected is used to stifle opposition and control the population.

- Lack of Oversight: In many cases, government surveillance practices lack proper oversight and accountability, leading to potential violations of individual rights. Without transparent policies and checks on government power, citizens may be subject to unwarranted surveillance.

- Erosion of Trust: The knowledge that the government may be monitoring personal data can erode trust between citizens and public institutions. This distrust can deter individuals from engaging with government services or participating in civic activities, ultimately undermining democracy.

IMPACT ON VULNERABLE POPULATIONS

- Disproportionate Effects: Marginalized communities often bear the brunt of surveillance practices. Factors such as race, socioeconomic status, and political beliefs can influence how individuals are monitored and treated by authorities.

- Targeted Surveillance: Vulnerable populations, including racial minorities and activists, may be subject to increased scrutiny and surveillance. For instance, law enforcement agencies may disproportionately monitor protests or gatherings related to social justice issues, leading to harassment and criminalization of legitimate dissent.

- Chilling Effects on Participation: The heightened risk of surveillance can discourage individuals from participating in civic engagement, activism, or community organizing. Fear of repercussions can lead to self-censorship, preventing marginalized voices from being heard and limiting the diversity of perspectives in public discourse.

- Exacerbation of Existing Inequalities: Surveillance practices can exacerbate existing social inequalities. Marginalized communities may have less access to legal protections and resources to challenge invasive surveillance practices, leading to a cycle of oppression and disenfranchisement.

SUMMARY

In this chapter, we have examined the security concerns associated with AI monitoring, including the risks of data breaches, the implications of government surveillance, and the disproportionate impact on vulnerable populations. Understanding these security concerns is crucial for recognizing the urgent need for robust regulatory frameworks that protect individual rights and foster accountability in data collection practices. The next chapter will explore the concept of data as a commodity, discussing how personal information is monetized and the broader implications for society.

MANIPULATION AND CONTROL

- Targeted Advertising: One of the most prominent uses of collected data is in targeted advertising, where companies analyze user behavior to deliver personalized ads. While this can enhance user experience by showing relevant products and services, it raises ethical concerns about manipulation. Users may be nudged toward purchases based on insights derived from their online activity, often without their explicit awareness.

- Behavioral Profiling: Companies can create detailed profiles of individuals based on their data, which can then be used to predict and influence behavior. These profiles allow marketers to tailor messages that exploit psychological triggers, potentially leading to impulsive buying decisions or reinforcing existing biases.

- Political Influence: Political campaigns increasingly leverage data analytics to target voters with tailored messages. The Cambridge Analytica scandal, where personal data from millions of Facebook users was used to influence the 2016 U.S. presidential election, exemplifies the risks of data misuse in the political sphere. By targeting specific demographics with tailored ads, campaigns can manipulate public perception and voter behavior, raising ethical concerns about informed consent and the integrity of democratic processes.

- Social Media Manipulation: Social media platforms can also be manipulated through the strategic use of algorithms that promote certain narratives or suppress dissenting voices. The spread of misinformation and "fake news" can be amplified through algorithmic bias, altering public perception and undermining informed decision-making.

PREDICTIVE POLICING AND BIAS

- Understanding Predictive Policing: Predictive policing uses data and algorithms to anticipate criminal activity and allocate law enforcement resources accordingly. While this approach aims to improve public safety, it raises significant ethical concerns.

- Potential for Bias: AI algorithms can inadvertently perpetuate or exacerbate existing biases in law enforcement. If historical data used to train these algorithms reflects systemic biases—such as over-policing of minority communities—the predictions made by these systems may disproportionately target those same communities.

- Racial Profiling and Discrimination: Predictive policing tools can lead to racial profiling, as law enforcement may focus on certain neighborhoods or demographics based on biased data. This practice undermines trust between communities and law enforcement and can result in unjust treatment of individuals based on their race or socioeconomic status.

- Lack of Accountability: The use of opaque algorithms in predictive policing raises concerns about accountability. Without transparency in how these algorithms operate, it becomes challenging to challenge or question their validity, leading to potential violations of civil rights.

SURVEILLANCE CAPITALISM

- Defining Surveillance Capitalism: Surveillance capitalism is a term coined by Shoshana Zuboff to describe a new economic system in which personal data is commodified and used to predict and influence behavior. In this framework, personal information is harvested without explicit consent and then used to create profit-driven business models.

- Data as an Asset: In surveillance capitalism, data is treated as a valuable asset that can be bought and sold. Companies collect vast amounts of user data, often without users' understanding or awareness, and leverage this information for financial gain. This commodification of personal information raises ethical questions about ownership and consent.

- Implications for Society: Surveillance capitalism has far-reaching implications for society, including:

- Erosion of Privacy: As companies increasingly rely on data collection to drive their business models, individuals may find their privacy further eroded, leading to a culture where constant surveillance is normalized.

- Manipulation of Public Discourse: By controlling the flow of information, companies can influence social norms, public opinion, and even political outcomes. This manipulation can undermine the democratic process and threaten the integrity of civil society.

- Devaluation of Human Autonomy: The pervasive collection and analysis of personal data can lead to a society where individuals feel less in control of their lives, as their choices and behaviors are shaped by algorithms designed to maximize engagement and profit.

SUMMARY

In this chapter, we have explored the various ways in which collected data can be misused, including manipulation through targeted advertising and political influence, the ethical concerns surrounding predictive policing and bias, and the concept of surveillance capitalism. Understanding these misuse possibilities is crucial for recognizing the urgent need for ethical standards, transparency, and regulatory frameworks that protect individual rights and foster accountability in data collection practices. The next chapter will focus on the call for regulation and transparency, discussing the current landscape and the necessary steps toward safeguarding privacy rights in the digital age.

CURRENT REGULATORY LANDSCAPE

- Overview of Existing Regulations:

- General Data Protection Regulation (GDPR): Enacted in the European Union in 2018, GDPR is one of the most comprehensive data privacy regulations globally. It imposes strict rules on data collection, processing, and storage, granting individuals rights over their personal data, including the right to access, rectify, and erase their information. Companies that fail to comply can face significant fines.

- California Consumer Privacy Act (CCPA): Effective from January 2020, the CCPA provides California residents with rights regarding their personal data, including the right to know what information is being collected, the right to delete personal information, and the right to opt out of the sale of their data. While it represents a significant step forward for consumer privacy in the U.S., its scope is limited to California residents and may not cover all forms of data processing.

- Other Regulations: Various countries have enacted their own privacy laws, such as Brazil's General Data Protection Law (LGPD) and Canada's Personal Information Protection and Electronic Documents Act (PIPEDA). However, the regulatory landscape remains fragmented, with different laws and standards across jurisdictions.

- Limitations of Existing Regulations:

- Enforcement Challenges: The effectiveness of regulations like GDPR and CCPA is often hampered by enforcement challenges. Regulatory bodies may lack the resources or authority to monitor compliance effectively, leading to inadequate protection for individuals.

- Scope and Coverage: Many existing regulations do not cover all types of data or organizations, leaving significant gaps in protection. For example, some laws may not apply to smaller companies or specific types of data processing.

- Lack of Consumer Awareness: Despite the existence of regulations, many individuals remain unaware of their rights under these laws. This lack of awareness can prevent them from exercising their rights and holding companies accountable.

THE NEED FOR NEW REGULATIONS

- Evolving Technological Landscape: As technology advances rapidly, existing regulations often struggle to keep pace with new developments in data collection and monitoring. The rise of AI, big data analytics, and IoT devices necessitates a reevaluation of regulatory frameworks to address emerging threats to privacy and personal sovereignty.

- Protecting Individuals from Invasive Monitoring: There is a pressing need for robust regulatory frameworks that:

- Establish clear guidelines for data collection and processing, ensuring that individuals have control over their personal information.

- Implement strict penalties for non-compliance to deter companies from engaging in invasive monitoring practices.

- Provide mechanisms for individuals to seek redress in cases of data breaches, misuse, or unauthorized access to their information.

- Global Cooperation: Given the borderless nature of the internet and data flows, international cooperation is crucial for developing consistent regulations that protect individuals worldwide. Collaborative efforts can help establish common standards and best practices that transcend national boundaries.

BEST PRACTICES FOR TRANSPARENCY

- Principles of Transparency: To foster trust and accountability, companies and governments should adopt best practices that prioritize transparency in data collection and processing:

- Clear Communication: Organizations should communicate their data collection practices in plain language, ensuring that individuals understand what data is being collected, how it will be used, and with whom it will be shared. Privacy policies should be concise, accessible, and free of legal jargon.

- Informed Consent: Obtaining informed consent from individuals before collecting their data is essential. Companies should provide users with clear options to opt in or out of data collection, along with easy-to-understand explanations of the implications of their choices.

- Regular Reporting: Organizations should be required to report regularly on their data collection practices, including the types of data collected, the purposes of collection, and any data breaches or misuse incidents. This reporting should be accessible to the public to enhance accountability.

- User Empowerment: Companies should implement user-friendly tools that allow individuals to manage their data, including options to view, edit, and delete their information. Providing transparency into data processing empowers users to make informed choices about their privacy.

SUMMARY

In this chapter, we have explored the current regulatory landscape regarding data privacy, highlighting existing regulations such as GDPR and CCPA, along with their limitations. We have argued for the necessity of new, robust regulatory frameworks to protect individuals from invasive monitoring and discussed best practices for transparency that organizations should adopt. The pressing need for enhanced regulations and transparency underscores the importance of safeguarding individual privacy rights in an increasingly data-driven world. The next chapter will focus on empowering individuals, providing practical tools and strategies for protecting personal privacy in the digital age.

EDUCATING THE PUBLIC

- Importance of Public Awareness: Raising awareness about AI monitoring and its implications is crucial for fostering an informed citizenry. Many individuals are unaware of the extent to which their data is collected, analyzed, and used, leading to a disconnect between technology use and the potential risks to personal privacy.

- Understanding Rights and Responsibilities: Education should empower individuals to understand their rights regarding data privacy and the responsibilities of companies and governments in protecting that data. Knowledge of privacy laws, such as GDPR and CCPA, can help individuals assert their rights and hold organizations accountable.

- Promoting Digital Literacy: Digital literacy programs can help individuals become more savvy about technology and data privacy. This includes understanding how algorithms work, recognizing phishing attempts, and knowing how to manage privacy settings on devices and applications.

- Community Engagement: Workshops, webinars, and community discussions can serve as platforms for sharing information about AI monitoring and privacy protections. Engaging local communities promotes collective awareness and encourages individuals to share their experiences and concerns.

- Practical Tips for Safeguarding Privacy:

- Adjust Privacy Settings: Encourage individuals to take the time to review and adjust privacy settings on their devices and applications. This includes limiting data sharing, disabling location services when not needed, and opting out of targeted advertising when possible.

- Use Virtual Private Networks (VPNs): VPNs encrypt internet traffic and mask IP addresses, providing an additional layer of privacy when browsing the web. This helps protect individuals from prying eyes, especially when using public Wi-Fi networks.

- Understand App Permissions: Individuals should carefully review app permissions before downloading and using applications. Many apps request access to data that is not necessary for their function. Encourage users to deny permissions that seem excessive or unrelated to the app's purpose.

- Regularly Update Software: Keeping devices and applications updated is essential for maintaining security. Software updates often include patches for vulnerabilities that could be exploited by cybercriminals.

- Utilize Privacy-Focused Tools: Recommend using privacy-focused search engines (like DuckDuckGo), secure messaging apps (like Signal or Telegram), and browser extensions (like Privacy Badger) that block tracking and enhance online privacy.

- Monitor Financial Accounts: Encourage individuals to regularly check bank and credit card statements for unauthorized transactions and to set up alerts for suspicious activities. This proactive approach can help detect identity theft early.

ADVOCACY AND ACTIVISM

- Engaging in Advocacy: Empowering individuals also means encouraging them to become advocates for stronger privacy protections. This can involve:

- Contacting Legislators: Individuals can reach out to their elected representatives to express their concerns about data privacy and urge them to support legislation that protects personal data.

- Joining Advocacy Groups: Various organizations focus on digital rights and privacy advocacy. Joining these groups can amplify individual voices and provide resources for collective action.

- Participating in Public Forums: Encourage readers to participate in public discussions, town halls, and community meetings to raise awareness about surveillance practices and advocate for transparency and accountability.

- Grassroots Movements: Highlight the power of grassroots movements in driving change. Many successful privacy initiatives have emerged from community-led efforts to demand better data protection practices and challenge invasive surveillance.

- Educating Others: Encourage individuals to share what they learn about AI monitoring and privacy protections with friends, family, and their broader communities. Raising collective awareness can create a ripple effect that fosters more informed discussions about data privacy.

SUMMARY

In this chapter, we have emphasized the importance of empowering individuals through education, practical tools for protecting privacy, and advocacy for stronger privacy protections. By fostering public awareness and engagement, individuals can take active roles in safeguarding their rights and influencing the regulatory landscape. The final chapter will reflect on the future of privacy in the digital age, discussing the ongoing challenges and the potential for creating a more respectful and secure digital environment for all.

EMERGING TECHNOLOGIES AND TRENDS

- Advancements in AI: The rapid development of artificial intelligence presents both opportunities and challenges for data privacy. AI technologies, including machine learning and natural language processing, are becoming increasingly sophisticated, enabling enhanced data analysis and automation.

- Enhanced Surveillance Capabilities: As AI systems evolve, their ability to monitor and analyze vast amounts of data will improve. This could lead to more intrusive surveillance practices, raising significant concerns about individual privacy and autonomy.

- Privacy-Enhancing Technologies: Conversely, advancements in technology also offer tools designed to protect privacy. Innovations such as differential privacy, federated learning, and homomorphic encryption aim to allow data analysis while minimizing the risk of exposing personal information. These technologies can help organizations leverage data without compromising user privacy.

- Regulatory Trends: As awareness of data privacy issues grows, there is an increasing push for stronger regulations globally. Countries are beginning to recognize the importance of safeguarding personal data and are implementing stricter regulations to protect citizens' privacy rights.

- International Cooperation: The future of privacy may also involve greater international cooperation to establish common standards for data protection, especially as data flows across borders. This collaborative approach can help create a more uniform regulatory environment, enhancing protections for individuals worldwide.

VISION FOR A PRIVACY-CONSCIOUS SOCIETY

- A Balanced Approach: Envisioning a future where technology and privacy coexist harmoniously requires a balanced approach that prioritizes individual rights while embracing innovation. This can be achieved through:

- Ethical Design Principles: Technology companies should adopt ethical design principles that prioritize user privacy from the outset. This includes implementing privacy by design, where products are built with privacy considerations integrated into their architecture.

- User Empowerment: Individuals should be empowered to make informed choices about their data. This includes having clear options to opt in or out of data collection, as well as accessible tools to manage their privacy preferences.

- Corporate Responsibility: Companies must recognize their role in protecting consumer data and adhere to high ethical standards in data collection and usage. This includes being transparent about data practices and prioritizing the security of user information.

- Community Engagement: A privacy-conscious society is one where communities actively engage in discussions about data privacy, surveillance, and individual rights. Encouraging civic engagement and fostering a culture of awareness can help build resilience against invasive practices.

- Individual Responsibility: Encourage readers to take personal responsibility for their data privacy. This includes:

- Educating themselves and others about data privacy issues, understanding their rights, and utilizing available tools to protect their information.

- Making conscious choices about the technologies they use, opting for services that prioritize privacy and ethical data practices.

- Advocacy and Participation: Stress the importance of advocacy in driving change. Readers are encouraged to:

- Engage with local and national organizations that focus on digital rights and privacy advocacy. Participation in campaigns and initiatives can amplify individual voices and influence policy changes.

- Reach out to legislators and policymakers, urging them to support and enact stronger privacy protections that reflect the needs and concerns of citizens.

- Supporting Privacy-Focused Policies: Encourage readers to advocate for policies that prioritize data privacy and ethical technology use. This can include:

- Supporting legislation that enhances data protection regulations, such as comprehensive privacy laws similar to GDPR.

- Promoting corporate accountability and transparency in data practices, ensuring that businesses prioritize user trust and ethical standards.

SUMMARY

In this final chapter, we have explored the future landscape of technology and data privacy, envisioning a society that balances innovation with individual rights. By embracing ethical design, user empowerment, and corporate responsibility, we can work toward a privacy-conscious society. The call to action emphasizes the importance of personal responsibility, advocacy, and supporting privacy-focused policies. As we navigate the complexities of the digital age, it is essential to remain vigilant and proactive in safeguarding our privacy rights, ensuring a future where technology serves humanity without compromising our fundamental freedoms.

The iPhone itself, independent of any third-party apps, has several built-in features and functionalities that involve AI monitoring and data collection, often without explicit user knowledge or awareness. Here are some ways this can occur:

1. SIRI AND VOICE RECOGNITION

- Always-On Listening: Siri, Apple's voice assistant, uses a feature called "always-on listening," which detects the wake word "Hey Siri." Although this functionality is intended to enhance user convenience, it means that the device is continuously listening for the activation phrase.

- Voice Data Processing: When you interact with Siri, your voice commands may be sent to Apple's servers for processing to improve voice recognition and AI understanding. While Apple states that it anonymizes this data, there are still privacy implications regarding how much data is collected and retained.

2. LOCATION SERVICES

- Background Location Tracking: The iPhone collects location data through GPS, Wi-Fi, Bluetooth, and cellular signals. Even if you are not using a specific app, the phone can continuously monitor your location for various system functions, such as improving location accuracy, providing location-based services, and enabling features like Find My iPhone.

- Geofencing: The device can create virtual boundaries to trigger specific actions based on your location, which may occur without direct user engagement or knowledge.

3. HEALTH AND FITNESS MONITORING

- Health App Data Collection: The iPhone can track health-related data through built-in sensors (like the accelerometer and gyroscope) and features like step counting and heart rate monitoring. This data is collected continuously and can be analyzed for insights into user activity levels, even if the user isn't actively using the Health app.

- Fitness Tracking: If enabled, fitness tracking features can monitor and record your movements throughout the day, contributing to a profile of your physical activity.

4. SYSTEM ANALYTICS AND DIAGNOSTICS

- Usage Data Collection: iPhones collect diagnostic and usage data to improve performance and identify issues. This data may include information about how the device is used, battery performance, and system errors. Users can opt out of sharing this data, but many may not be aware of its existence.

- Crash Reports: When apps crash or encounter errors, the iPhone can automatically send crash reports to Apple, which includes information about the app state and system performance at the time of the crash.

5. PERSONALIZATION AND SUGGESTIONS

- On-Device AI Processing: The iPhone uses on-device AI to analyze user behavior and preferences, leading to personalized suggestions in various areas, such as app recommendations, Siri suggestions, and predictive text. This analysis occurs without user intervention.

- Spotlight Search: The device may monitor usage patterns to enhance search functionality, providing relevant search results based on your interactions with apps and files, even if you're not actively searching.

6. DATA SYNCING WITH ICLOUD

- iCloud Backup: The iPhone can back up data to iCloud, which includes app data, settings, and device information. This process can occur automatically, and users may not be fully aware of the extent of what is being backed up.

- Location-Based Services in iCloud: Features like Find My iPhone rely on location data, which is continuously collected and synced with iCloud, even when not actively used.

7. APPLE'S ECOSYSTEM INTEGRATION

- Cross-Device Data Sharing: If you use multiple Apple devices, data can be shared across the ecosystem. For example, your iPhone can communicate with your iPad, Apple Watch, or Mac to provide a seamless experience. This integration can involve data collection and sharing without explicit user knowledge.

While many of these features are designed to enhance user experience and improve device functionality, they also raise privacy concerns regarding the extent of data collection and monitoring. Users should regularly review their privacy settings, disable unnecessary features, and be mindful of the data they share with the device to mitigate potential privacy risks. Understanding how these built-in functionalities work can help users make more informed choices about their privacy on an iPhone.

AI MONITORING ON AN IPHONE

AI monitoring on an iPhone can refer to various data collection practices and surveillance techniques utilized by apps, services, and even the operating system itself. While many of these practices aim to enhance user experience or provide valuable services, they can also occur without explicit user consent or awareness. Here are some common ways AI monitoring can happen on an iPhone:

1. LOCATION TRACKING

- Background Location Services: Many apps request access to your location data, which can be tracked even when the app is not actively in use. For instance, fitness apps, navigation services, and social media platforms may track your location to offer personalized services or targeted advertising.

- Geofencing: Apps can create geofences that trigger notifications or actions based on your location. This may involve tracking your movements without your explicit knowledge.

2. APP PERMISSIONS

- Microphone and Camera Access: Some apps may request permission to access your microphone or camera. If granted, these apps can potentially record audio or video without you being aware. This can be particularly concerning if the app's privacy policy is not transparent.

- Data Sharing: Apps may collect and share data from your device, such as contact lists, photos, and usage statistics, raising concerns about how this data is used or sold.

3. USAGE DATA COLLECTION

- Analytics Tracking: Many apps and services track how you interact with them, collecting data on app usage, screen time, and interactions. This data can be used to improve services or targeted advertising but may be done without your explicit awareness.

- Behavioral Profiling: By analyzing your usage patterns and preferences, companies can create detailed profiles to predict your behavior and tailor content or advertisements to you.

4. BACKGROUND APP REFRESH

- Continuous Data Collection: Background app refresh allows apps to update content in the background. This means apps can collect data even when you are not actively using them, contributing to ongoing monitoring.

5. ARTIFICIAL INTELLIGENCE ALGORITHMS

- Predictive Text and Suggestions: AI algorithms analyze your typing patterns, interests, and previous interactions to provide predictive text suggestions or personalized content. While this feature is designed to enhance user experience, it involves ongoing data analysis.

- Voice Assistants: Siri, Apple's voice assistant, continuously listens for the "Hey Siri" command, which can raise concerns about privacy and the extent of data collection. Although voice recordings are typically processed on the device, there is still potential for data to be stored and analyzed.

6. THIRD-PARTY TRACKING

- Cookies and Trackers in Apps: Some apps may use third-party tracking technologies to monitor user behavior across different apps and websites. This can lead to the creation of detailed profiles that are sold to advertisers.

- Advertising Networks: Many apps rely on advertising networks that collect data on user behavior to serve targeted ads. This involves the collection of information across multiple platforms and devices.

7. DATA BACKUPS

- iCloud and Data Storage: Data collected from your device can be backed up to iCloud, which includes app data, settings, and usage information. While this is useful for data recovery, it also means that your information is stored on Apple's servers and can be accessed by Apple or third parties under certain conditions.

While many of these monitoring practices are designed to improve user experience and provide personalized services, they also raise significant privacy concerns. Users may not always be aware of the extent of data collection and monitoring occurring on their devices. To mitigate these concerns, it is essential to regularly review app permissions, adjust privacy settings, and stay informed about data privacy practices.

AI monitoring and reporting on an Android phone can occur independently of third-party apps through various built-in features and system functionalities. These mechanisms may collect data and monitor user behavior without explicit user knowledge or consent. Here are some ways this can happen:

1. SYSTEM SERVICES AND FEATURES

- Google Services Integration: Android phones are often tightly integrated with Google services. Features like Google Assistant, Google Maps, and Google Search collect and analyze user data for personalization and functionality. Even when not actively using these services, data can be collected in the background.

- Location Services: Android devices continuously monitor location using GPS, Wi-Fi, and cellular data. This can happen even when location-based apps are not in use. Users may have location history enabled, allowing Google to track and save their movements over time.

2. VOICE RECOGNITION

- Always-On Listening: The Google Assistant feature that listens for the "Hey Google" command means that the microphone is actively monitoring for this phrase. While this is intended to provide a responsive experience, it can lead to concerns about what data is being captured before the command is activated.

- Voice Command Analysis: When users interact with Google Assistant, their voice commands may be sent to Google's servers for processing. This helps improve the accuracy of voice recognition but raises questions about data retention and privacy.

3. SYSTEM ANALYTICS AND DIAGNOSTICS

- Usage and Diagnostic Data: Android devices collect diagnostic and usage data to improve performance and user experience. This can involve data on app usage, battery life, crash reports, and system performance. Users typically consent to this data collection during the setup process but may not fully understand its extent.

- Crash and Error Reports: When an app crashes or experiences an error, Android can automatically send reports to Google. This data can include information about the device state, installed apps, and interactions leading up to the crash.

4. PERSONALIZATION AND SUGGESTIONS

- On-Device AI Processing: Android uses built-in AI algorithms to analyze user behavior for personalized suggestions, such as app recommendations or predictive typing. This analysis occurs on-device and can happen without active user engagement or knowledge.

- Smart Suggestions: Features like Smart Reply or predictive text analyze your typing patterns and email responses, enhancing user experience but also collecting data on user behavior without explicit awareness.

5. DATA SYNCING AND BACKUP

- Google Account Sync: If a user is signed into a Google account, various data types (contacts, calendar events, and usage data) can be automatically synced to Google's servers. This happens in the background and can include data from built-in apps, contributing to a detailed user profile.

- Automatic Backups: Android devices can automatically back up app data and settings to Google Drive. This process can occur without direct user intervention, leading to potential data collection without explicit awareness.

6. DEVICE HEALTH AND PERFORMANCE MONITORING

- Device Health Services: Android includes features that monitor device health, such as battery usage statistics and system performance metrics. This data can be collected and sent to Google to help optimize future updates and service improvements.

- Network Monitoring: The device may monitor network activity and connectivity to improve performance. This includes tracking data usage patterns that can inform how the device connects to Wi-Fi or cellular networks.

7. DEVICE SETTINGS AND PERMISSIONS

- Default Permissions: During the initial setup of an Android device, users often grant permissions for various system services, which can include data collection for location, usage statistics, and diagnostics. Users may not fully understand the implications of these permissions.

AI monitoring on Android devices can occur independently of any third-party apps through built-in features, system services, and integration with Google services. While many of these functionalities aim to enhance user experience and device performance, they can also raise significant privacy concerns regarding the extent of monitoring and data collection. Users should proactively review their privacy settings, manage permissions, and understand the implications of various features to better protect their privacy.

AI monitoring on an Android device can encompass various data collection and tracking practices that occur without the explicit knowledge or consent of the user. Here are several ways in which AI monitoring can happen on Android devices:

1. LOCATION TRACKING

- Background Location Services: Android devices frequently use GPS, Wi-Fi, and cellular data to provide location-based services. Apps may request location access, and even when closed, the device can still track your location for features like geofencing, navigation, or location-based reminders.

- Google Location History: If enabled, Android devices may automatically save location history to your Google account, which can be accessed across devices. This feature can track your movements without direct interaction.

2. VOICE ASSISTANTS AND RECOGNITION

- Google Assistant: Similar to Siri on iOS, Google Assistant is always listening for the wake phrase "Hey Google." While this feature is designed for ease of use, it does mean that the device is continuously listening for commands.

- Voice Data Processing: Voice commands given to Google Assistant may be sent to Google's servers for processing, where they are analyzed to improve the assistant's performance. Users may not be aware of how long this data is retained or how it is used.

3. APP PERMISSIONS AND BACKGROUND ACTIVITY

- App Permissions: Many apps on Android may request permissions to access sensitive data, such as contacts, camera, microphone, and location. Some apps may continue to collect data even when they are not in active use, depending on the permissions granted.

- Background Activity: Apps can run in the background and may collect usage data or monitor behavior even when not actively being used. This includes collecting information on how often you open certain apps and your interactions within them.

4. USAGE DATA COLLECTION

- Analytics and Diagnostics: Android devices collect usage data and diagnostics to improve performance and user experience. This data may include information about how apps are used, battery performance, and system errors. Users may not explicitly consent to this data collection.

- Google Services Data: Google services (like Google Maps, Google Search, and YouTube) collect data on your interactions, preferences, and search history, contributing to targeted advertising and personalized content delivery.

5. BEHAVIORAL PROFILING

- Ad Personalization: Android devices often utilize advertising IDs to track user behavior across apps and websites, allowing for targeted advertising based on user interests. This process may occur without the user's full awareness of how their interactions are being tracked and analyzed.

- Google's Machine Learning Models: Google uses data collected from Android devices to train its machine learning models, which can analyze patterns and make predictions about user behavior, preferences, and needs.

6. DATA SYNCING AND BACKUP

- Google Account Sync: If you use a Google account on your Android device, data such as contacts, calendar events, and app data may be automatically synced to Google's servers. This can include data collected by various apps and services, contributing to a detailed profile of your activities.

- Backup Services: Android devices can backup app data and settings to Google Drive. This process may happen automatically and without explicit user knowledge, depending on the device settings.

- Third-Party SDKs: Many apps use third-party software development kits (SDKs) for analytics and advertising, which can track user behavior and collect data without direct user consent. This data can be shared with advertisers and used for targeted marketing.

- Cookies and Tracking Technologies: When using web browsers on Android, cookies and other tracking technologies may be used to monitor browsing behavior and gather data for advertising purposes.

- Device Health Monitoring: Android devices may collect data on device performance and health metrics, including battery usage, storage capacity, and system errors. This data can help optimize device performance but may also be collected and analyzed without user awareness.

- Network Activity Monitoring: Your Android device may monitor network activity to improve connectivity and performance, potentially collecting data about your internet usage patterns.

AI monitoring on Android devices can occur through a variety of built-in features and functionalities that collect data without explicit user knowledge. While many of these features aim to enhance user experience, they also raise significant privacy concerns regarding the extent of monitoring and data collection. Users should regularly review app permissions, adjust privacy settings, and stay informed about data privacy practices to mitigate potential risks. Understanding how these monitoring practices work can empower users to make informed choices about their privacy on Android devices.

Certainly! Here's a revised version that emphasizes the role of AI in monitoring on a Windows computer, highlighting how it contributes to data collection and user behavior tracking without explicit user knowledge.

AI MONITORING ON WINDOWS COMPUTERS WITHOUT USER KNOWLEDGE

AI monitoring on a Windows computer can occur through various built-in features and system processes that leverage artificial intelligence to collect data and track user behavior. Here are several ways this can happen:

1. WINDOWS SERVICES AND FEATURES

- Cortana and Voice Recognition: Microsoft's digital assistant, Cortana, uses AI-driven voice recognition technology that listens for a wake word. This continuous listening capability allows Cortana to provide assistance but raises concerns about what data is captured before activation. AI algorithms analyze voice commands to improve recognition accuracy, which involves sending voice data to Microsoft's servers for processing.

- Telemetry Data Collection: Windows operating systems utilize AI to analyze telemetry data to improve system performance and enhance user experience. This data includes hardware configurations, software usage patterns, system errors, and performance metrics. While users can configure some telemetry settings, AI processes often operate in the background to collect and analyze data without explicit consent.

2. BACKGROUND APPLICATIONS AND PROCESSES

- Pre-installed Applications: Windows comes with several pre-installed applications (like OneDrive and Microsoft Edge) that use AI analytics to monitor usage data and user interactions. These applications may collect data in the background, leveraging AI to optimize their performance and user engagement without clear user awareness.

- Background App Activity: Many applications on Windows have permissions to run in the background, allowing them to collect data even when not actively in use. AI is often employed to analyze this usage data, which can include tracking user interactions and preferences to create user profiles for personalization.

3. INTERNET BROWSING AND ONLINE ACTIVITY

- Browser Tracking: Web browsers on Windows, such as Microsoft Edge, utilize AI algorithms to track online behavior through cookies, browsing history, and search queries. This data is analyzed to deliver targeted advertising and personalized content, often without the user's explicit knowledge of the extent of monitoring.

- Ad Personalization: Windows systems may use AI to create personalized advertising experiences by analyzing user behavior and interactions across various applications and websites. AI-driven algorithms help serve ads tailored to user interests, which can occur without the user being fully aware of the data being collected.

---

4. MICROSOFT ACCOUNT INTEGRATION

- Cloud Syncing: If users are signed into a Microsoft account, various settings, preferences, and data (like browsing history and app settings) can be automatically synced to Microsoft's servers. AI plays a role in determining which data is relevant for syncing and how to optimize this process, often occurring without users realizing the full extent of the data being shared.

- Activity History: Windows may track user activity history across devices if certain features are enabled. AI algorithms analyze this data to provide insights into application usage and file access, integrating with features like Timeline to enhance user experience while potentially infringing on privacy.

5. SYSTEM UPDATES AND DIAGNOSTICS

- Automatic Updates: Windows frequently downloads and installs updates in the background to ensure optimal performance and security. AI is used to analyze system behavior and user interactions to determine what updates are necessary, sometimes without the user's awareness of the data being collected in the process.

- Error Reporting: When applications crash or encounter errors, Windows may automatically send error reports to Microsoft. AI analyzes these reports to identify patterns and diagnose issues, which can include diagnostic information and usage statistics, contributing to privacy concerns.

6. REMOTE ACCESS AND MONITORING

- Remote Desktop Services: If enabled, the Remote Desktop feature allows other users or administrators to access your computer remotely. AI can enhance this capability by analyzing user permissions and access patterns, but it also raises concerns about unauthorized access and monitoring.

- Microsoft Defender and Security Features: Built-in security features like Microsoft Defender use AI to monitor system behavior for potential threats. While critical for security, this monitoring involves analyzing user behavior and network activity, sometimes without explicit user consent.

- Cloud Backups: Windows can automatically back up files to OneDrive or other cloud services. AI can determine which files are most critical for backup based on usage patterns, and this process may occur without explicit user actions, leading to concerns about what files and data are being stored and shared.

AI monitoring on a Windows computer occurs through various built-in features, system processes, and integration with Microsoft services. While many of these functionalities aim to enhance user experience, improve system performance, and ensure security, they can also raise significant privacy concerns regarding the extent of data collection and monitoring. Users should regularly review their privacy settings, manage permissions, and stay informed about data privacy practices to mitigate potential risks. Understanding the role of AI in these monitoring practices can empower users to make more informed choices about their privacy on Windows devices.

Background

The Cambridge Analytica scandal emerged in 2018 as a significant political data controversy, spotlighting how personal data from millions of Facebook users was harvested without their consent for targeted political advertising. Cambridge Analytica, a data analytics firm, was involved in various political campaigns, including the 2016 U.S. presidential election and the Brexit referendum in the United Kingdom.

DATA HARVESTING PROCESS

1. Facebook App Exploitation: Cambridge Analytica utilized a personality quiz app called "This Is Your Digital Life," developed by researcher Aleksandr Kogan. The app was designed to gather information about users' personalities based on their responses to questions.

2. User Consent Misuse: When users signed up for the quiz, they granted permissions for the app to access their Facebook profiles. However, the app also collected data from users' friends, allowing Kogan to harvest information from approximately 87 million Facebook accounts without those friends' explicit consent.

3. Data Profiling: The data collected included personal details, interests, likes, and interactions, which were then used to create detailed psychological profiles of users. These profiles enabled Cambridge Analytica to categorize individuals based on personality traits and political preferences.

TARGETED ADVERTISING

1. Microtargeting: With the extensive data profiling, Cambridge Analytica employed microtargeting strategies to deliver highly specific advertisements to users. This approach allowed political campaigns to tailor messages that resonated with particular demographics, utilizing insights derived from the psychological profiles.

2. Influencing Behavior: The targeted ads were designed to sway voter opinions and behaviors by appealing to emotions, fears, and motivations identified in the data profiles. This included negative advertising against opponents and content aimed at galvanizing particular voter bases.

ETHICAL AND LEGAL IMPLICATIONS

1. Informed Consent Violations: The scandal raised profound ethical questions about informed consent. Users were largely unaware that their data was being collected and used for political purposes, highlighting significant gaps in privacy protections.

2. Regulatory Repercussions: The fallout from the scandal led to increased scrutiny of data privacy regulations. It prompted investigations by various governments and regulatory bodies, including the U.S. Federal Trade Commission (FTC) and the UK Information Commissioner's Office. Facebook faced fines and was pressured to implement stricter data privacy measures.

3. Public Backlash: The scandal ignited widespread public outrage over data privacy and the misuse of personal information. It led to calls for greater transparency and accountability in how companies handle user data, culminating in movements advocating for stronger data protection laws.

CONCLUSION

The Cambridge Analytica scandal serves as a cautionary tale about the risks associated with data profiling and targeted advertising. It illustrates how personal data can be harvested and exploited without user consent, raising critical concerns about privacy, ethics, and the integrity of democratic processes. This case underscores the need for robust data protection regulations and consumer awareness to prevent similar incidents in the future. The implications of the scandal continue to influence discussions around data privacy, user consent, and the role of technology in shaping public opinion.

BACKGROUND

The General Data Protection Regulation (GDPR) became enforceable on May 25, 2018, establishing a comprehensive framework for data protection and privacy for individuals within the European Union (EU) and the European Economic Area (EEA). The regulation aimed to enhance individuals' control over their personal data and to simplify the regulatory environment for international business by unifying data protection laws across Europe.

KEY PROVISIONS OF GDPR

1. Data Subject Rights: GDPR introduced several rights for individuals, including the right to access personal data, the right to rectification, the right to erasure (the "right to be forgotten"), the right to data portability, and the right to object to processing.

2. Consent Requirements: Companies must obtain clear and explicit consent from users before collecting, processing, or storing their personal data. This requires organizations to provide transparent information about data usage and to allow users to withdraw consent easily.

3. Data Protection Officers (DPOs): Organizations that process large amounts of personal data or sensitive data are required to appoint a

Data Protection Officer responsible for overseeing compliance with GDPR.

4. Breach Notification: Companies must notify relevant authorities and affected individuals within 72 hours of discovering a data breach, enhancing accountability and transparency.

5. Fines and Penalties: GDPR established significant penalties for non-compliance, allowing for fines of up to €20 million or 4% of a company's global annual turnover, whichever is higher.

IMPACT ON BUSINESSES

1. Compliance Costs: Many organizations faced substantial costs in implementing GDPR compliance measures. This included legal consultations, technology upgrades, training staff, and establishing new data processing protocols. Small and medium-sized enterprises (SMEs) particularly struggled with the financial burden of compliance.

2. Operational Changes: Companies had to overhaul their data management practices to ensure transparency and accountability. This often involved revising privacy policies, conducting data audits, and implementing new consent mechanisms. Organizations also had to review their vendor contracts to ensure compliance throughout their supply chains.

3. Increased Accountability: GDPR placed greater responsibility on organizations to demonstrate compliance. This shift required businesses to document all data processing activities, conduct regular risk assessments, and establish clear procedures for handling data subject requests.

4. Impact on Marketing Practices: The regulation fundamentally changed how businesses approached marketing and data collection. Companies could no longer rely on implicit consent or vague terms of service. Marketers had to ensure that their practices aligned with GDPR requirements, which often led to a reduction in the amount of data collected for targeted advertising.

5. Cross-Border Data Transfers: GDPR imposed strict regulations on transferring personal data outside the EU. Organizations had to ensure that any third countries receiving data provided adequate protection, which complicated international operations and partnerships.

CHALLENGES FACED

1. Complexity of Compliance: Many organizations struggled to fully understand and interpret the intricate requirements of GDPR. This complexity led to confusion and inconsistent implementation across different sectors.

2. Resistance to Change: Some companies faced internal resistance to the changes required for compliance, particularly if it affected established practices or required significant shifts in company culture.

3. Staff Training: Ensuring that employees were adequately trained on GDPR requirements was a significant challenge. Organizations needed to invest time and resources into educating staff about data protection responsibilities.

4. Evolving Regulatory Landscape: As GDPR set a precedent for data protection worldwide, organizations also faced uncertainty as new regulations emerged in other jurisdictions. Companies had to stay informed about how these developments would affect their operations.

CONCLUSION

The implementation of the General Data Protection Regulation (GDPR) marked a significant shift in data protection practices for businesses operating in the EU. While it presented challenges, particularly in terms of compliance costs and operational changes, GDPR also fostered a greater emphasis on data protection and consumer rights. The regulation has influenced global conversations about data privacy and has prompted many organizations outside the EU to adopt similar practices to remain competitive and compliant. The lessons learned from GDPR's implementation continue to shape the landscape of data protection, emphasizing the importance of transparency, accountability, and respect for individual privacy.

In an era characterized by rapid technological advancements, it is essential to educate the public about the implications of AI monitoring on privacy and personal sovereignty. As artificial intelligence becomes increasingly integrated into daily life—through smartphones, smart home devices, and online services—understanding how these technologies operate and the data they collect is vital for maintaining individual rights. Here's how we can effectively achieve this goal:

RAISING AWARENESS

1. Information Campaigns: Launch targeted campaigns that highlight the risks associated with AI monitoring and data collection. Utilizing various media platforms—social media, podcasts, blogs, and webinars—can help disseminate information to a broad audience.

2. Workshops and Seminars: Organize community workshops and seminars to discuss data privacy, AI technologies, and their implications. These events can provide a platform for experts to explain complex concepts in accessible terms, enabling participants to ask questions and engage in discussions.

3. Case Studies: Use real-world examples, such as the Cambridge Analytica scandal or the implications of GDPR, to illustrate the potential consequences of data misuse and the importance of regulatory frameworks. Case studies can make abstract concepts more tangible and relatable.

1. Providing Resources: Create accessible resources, such as guides, infographics, and toolkits, that help individuals understand their rights regarding data privacy. This includes information on how to manage privacy settings, recognize data collection practices, and take action when their rights are violated.

2. Encouraging Critical Thinking: Foster critical thinking skills by encouraging individuals to question the technologies they use. Prompt users to consider what data is being collected, how it is being used, and whether they are comfortable with the permissions they grant.

3. Promoting Digital Literacy: Incorporate digital literacy programs in schools and community organizations, focusing on understanding digital footprints, recognizing phishing scams, and safeguarding personal information. An informed citizenry is more likely to take proactive measures to protect their privacy.

1. Encouraging Advocacy: Empower individuals to advocate for greater regulation and transparency in the digital landscape. This can involve writing to lawmakers, participating in public consultations, and supporting organizations that fight for digital rights and privacy protections.

2. Supporting Legislation: Highlight the importance of supporting robust data protection legislation, such as the General Data Protection Regulation (GDPR) in the EU, and similar frameworks in other jurisdictions. Encourage citizens to stay informed about proposed legislation and to engage with their representatives on these issues.

3. Building Alliances: Foster collaborations between civil society organizations, tech companies, and policymakers to create a shared vision for a transparent and accountable digital ecosystem. Joint initiatives can amplify voices advocating for individual rights and privacy protections.

1. Creating Community Forums: Establish community forums—both online and offline—where individuals can discuss their concerns about AI monitoring and privacy issues. These spaces can facilitate dialogue and collective action, empowering citizens to share experiences and strategies for advocacy.

2. Utilizing Social Media: Leverage social media platforms to create awareness and mobilize action. Encourage individuals to share their perspectives, experiences, and knowledge, fostering a community of informed advocates for privacy rights.

3. Continuous Learning: Emphasize that the landscape of technology and privacy is constantly evolving. Encourage ongoing education and engagement with emerging issues related to AI monitoring, data privacy, and personal sovereignty, ensuring that citizens remain informed and prepared to advocate for their rights.

As technology continues to evolve, fostering an informed and engaged citizenry will be crucial in shaping a future that respects individual rights and freedoms. By effectively educating the public about the implications of AI monitoring, empowering individuals with knowledge, and encouraging advocacy for greater regulation and transparency, we can collectively strive for a digital landscape that prioritizes privacy and personal sovereignty. The journey towards a more equitable and respectful technological future begins with awareness and action, ensuring that individuals remain at the forefront of the conversation about their rights in the digital age.

These are suggested comprehensive regulations for AI data collection and its use, along with the anticipated impact of each regulation. These regulations aim to promote transparency, accountability, and user rights in the context of data collection and AI technologies.

1. INFORMED CONSENT REQUIREMENTS

 - Description: Mandate that organizations obtain explicit and informed consent from users before collecting, processing, or sharing their personal data. This includes clear communication about what data is being collected, how it will be used, and who it will be shared with.

  - Impact:

   - Empowers individuals to make informed decisions about their data.

   - Reduces the likelihood of data misuse and exploitation.

   - Encourages companies to be more transparent about their data practices.

2. DATA MINIMIZATION PRINCIPLE

- Description: Require organizations to collect only the data that is necessary for the specified purpose and to avoid excessive data collection. This includes limiting the duration for which data is stored.

- Impact:

  - Reduces the amount of personal data at risk of exposure in the event of a data breach.

  - Encourages organizations to focus on essential data, improving overall data management practices.

  - Helps build user trust by demonstrating respect for privacy.

3. RIGHT TO ACCESS AND PORTABILITY

- Description: Grant individuals the right to access their personal data held by organizations and to obtain a copy in a structured, commonly used, and machine-readable format. This includes the ability to transfer their data to another provider.

- Impact:

  - Enhances user control over personal data and fosters trust in organizations.

  - Encourages competition among service providers by enabling easier data transfer.

  - Promotes accountability by requiring organizations to maintain accurate and accessible data.

4. TRANSPARENCY AND ALGORITHMIC ACCOUNTABILITY

- Description: Require organizations to disclose how AI algorithms function, including the data sources, decision-making processes, and potential biases. This includes periodic audits of AI systems for fairness and compliance.

  - Impact:

  - Increases public understanding of AI technologies and their implications.

  - Helps identify and mitigate biases in AI systems, promoting fairness and equity.

  - Encourages organizations to adopt ethical practices in AI development and deployment.

5. DATA BREACH NOTIFICATION REQUIREMENTS

- Description: Mandate that organizations notify affected individuals and relevant authorities within a specified timeframe (e.g., 72 hours) of discovering a data breach that compromises personal data.

  - Impact:

  - Ensures timely awareness of data breaches, allowing individuals to take protective measures.

  - Promotes accountability among organizations regarding data protection.

- Helps build public trust by demonstrating a commitment to transparency and responsibility.

6. ESTABLISHMENT OF DATA PROTECTION OFFICERS (DPOS)

- Description: Require organizations that process significant amounts of personal data to appoint a Data Protection Officer responsible for overseeing compliance with data protection regulations and acting as a point of contact for users.

- Impact:

- Enhances organizational accountability regarding data protection practices.

- Provides users with a clear channel for addressing concerns and inquiries.

- Encourages proactive identification and mitigation of privacy risks.

7. PRIVACY BY DESIGN AND DEFAULT

- Description: Mandate that organizations implement data protection measures from the outset of any project involving personal data, ensuring that privacy is integrated into the development process. Default settings should prioritize user privacy.

- Impact:

- Promotes a proactive approach to data protection, reducing the risk of privacy violations.

- Encourages innovation in developing privacy-centric technologies and practices.

- Builds user confidence in products and services that prioritize privacy.

8. REGULAR AUDITS AND COMPLIANCE CHECKS

- Description: Require organizations to undergo regular audits and compliance checks to ensure adherence to data protection regulations and accountability in AI practices.

- Impact:

- Helps identify non-compliance and areas for improvement in data protection practices.

- Increases transparency and fosters a culture of accountability within organizations.

- Deters organizations from engaging in unethical data practices due to the risk of scrutiny.

9. USER EMPOWERMENT AND EDUCATION INITIATIVES

- Description: Implement programs to educate users about their rights regarding data privacy, the implications of AI monitoring, and how to manage their personal information effectively.

- Impact:

- Empowers individuals to take control of their data and make informed decisions.

- Fosters a culture of privacy awareness and advocacy among the public.

- Encourages organizations to prioritize user education as part of their data protection strategies.

10. CROSS-BORDER DATA TRANSFER REGULATIONS

- Description: Establish clear guidelines for the transfer of personal data across borders, ensuring that adequate data protection measures are in place in the receiving countries.

- Impact:

- Protects individuals' data when it is transferred to countries with less stringent data privacy laws.

- Promotes international cooperation on data protection standards.

- Reduces the risk of data exploitation in jurisdictions lacking robust protections.

These comprehensive regulations aim to create a balanced framework that protects individual privacy while allowing for the responsible use of AI and data collection. By implementing these measures, society can foster greater trust in technology, ensure accountability among organizations, and empower individuals to take control of their personal data. As technology continues to evolve, these regulations will be essential in addressing emerging challenges in the digital landscape and safeguarding individual rights and freedoms.

Addressing the overreach of AI data collection on cell phones and systems operated by companies such as Facebook, Amazon, Apple, Microsoft, and others requires a multi-faceted approach that includes legislative action, technological solutions, user education, and advocacy. Below are several strategies that can be implemented to mitigate the risks associated with excessive data collection:

1. STRENGTHENING DATA PROTECTION REGULATIONS

- Advocate for Comprehensive Data Privacy Laws: Support the development and enforcement of robust data protection legislation similar to the General Data Protection Regulation (GDPR) in the EU. This includes regulations that require explicit consent for data collection, provide users with rights to access and delete their data, and impose penalties for non-compliance.

- Implement Stronger Consent Requirements: Push for regulations that require clear, informed, and unambiguous consent from users before collecting or processing their data. Users should be informed about what data is being collected, how it will be used, and with whom it will be shared.

2. ENHANCING TRANSPARENCY AND ACCOUNTABILITY

- Demand Transparency Reports: Encourage companies to publish regular transparency reports detailing their data collection practices, including what data is collected, how it is used, and any third parties it is shared with. This can help hold companies accountable for their data practices.

- AI Algorithm Audits: Advocate for regular audits of AI algorithms and data collection practices to ensure compliance with ethical standards and to identify potential biases or misuse of data.

3. EMPOWERING USERS

- Promote User Education: Increase awareness among users about the implications of data collection, including how to manage privacy settings on their devices and applications. Educational initiatives can help users make informed decisions about their data.

- Encourage Use of Privacy Tools: Promote the use of privacy-focused tools and applications, such as virtual private networks (VPNs), ad blockers, and privacy-centric browsers, to help users limit data tracking and enhance their online privacy.

4. SUPPORTING PRIVACY-CENTRIC ALTERNATIVES

- Encourage Development of Alternatives: Support the development and use of privacy-centric alternatives to mainstream services. For example, promote search engines like DuckDuckGo that do not track user data, or messaging apps like Signal that prioritize end-to-end encryption.

- Foster Competition in the Market: Advocate for policies that encourage competition in the tech industry, allowing smaller companies that prioritize privacy to thrive alongside larger corporations.

5. IMPLEMENTING TECHNOLOGICAL SOLUTIONS

- Improve Device Settings: Encourage smartphone manufacturers to offer enhanced privacy settings that enable users to easily control what data is collected and shared by their devices and applications. This includes options for limiting background data access and disabling unnecessary permissions.

- Develop Privacy-Enhancing Technologies: Support research and development of technologies that enhance user privacy, such as decentralized data storage solutions that give users greater control over their personal information.

6. ADVOCACY AND PUBLIC PRESSURE

- Engage in Advocacy Campaigns: Join or support advocacy groups focused on digital rights and privacy protection. Collective action can amplify the call for stronger regulations and ethical practices in data collection.

- Raise Public Awareness: Utilize media campaigns to raise public awareness about the risks of excessive data collection and the importance of protecting personal privacy. Highlighting real-world examples of data misuse can galvanize public support for change.

7. LEGAL ACTION AND LITIGATION

- Support Class Action Lawsuits: Encourage individuals to participate in or support class-action lawsuits against companies that engage in deceptive data practices or fail to protect user data adequately. Legal action can serve as a powerful tool to hold corporations accountable.

- Challenge Unlawful Practices: Provide resources and support for individuals to challenge unlawful data collection practices through legal channels, advocating for their rights under existing privacy laws.

Combating the overreach of AI data collection on cell phones and systems operated by companies such as Facebook, Amazon, Apple, Microsoft, and others requires a comprehensive strategy that combines regulatory reform, technological solutions, user empowerment, and public advocacy. By working together across these areas, individuals, organizations, and policymakers can promote a more privacy-respecting digital landscape that safeguards personal rights and freedoms. As technology continues to evolve, ongoing vigilance and engagement will be essential to ensure that data collection practices remain ethical and transparent.

Addressing government overreach in AI tracking and surveillance requires a strategic approach that emphasizes accountability, transparency, and respect for individual rights. Here are several strategies that can be implemented to effectively confront and mitigate government surveillance practices:

1. ADVOCACY FOR STRONGER DATA PROTECTION LAWS

- Promote Legislative Reform: Advocate for the introduction and strengthening of data protection laws that clearly define the limits of government surveillance and establish strict guidelines for data collection, storage, and usage. This includes ensuring that any surveillance practices are proportionate, necessary, and subject to oversight.

- Support Privacy Rights Legislation: Encourage the development of laws that specifically protect citizens' privacy rights against unwarranted surveillance, such as the right to be informed about data collection and the right to challenge unlawful surveillance practices.

2. FOSTER PUBLIC AWARENESS AND EDUCATION

- Raise Awareness: Conduct campaigns to inform the public about the implications of government surveillance and the potential risks to privacy and civil liberties. Use various platforms, including social media, community forums, and educational workshops, to disseminate information.

- Promote Digital Literacy: Educate citizens about their rights regarding surveillance and data privacy, including how to protect their personal information and recognize when their data may be subject to government scrutiny.

3. ENCOURAGE TRANSPARENCY AND ACCOUNTABILITY

- Demand Transparency Reports: Advocate for governments to publish regular transparency reports detailing their surveillance activities, including the types of data collected, the legal justifications for surveillance, and the number of individuals affected. This can help hold authorities accountable for their actions.

- Establish Oversight Mechanisms: Call for the creation of independent oversight bodies with the authority to review government surveillance practices. These bodies should have the power to investigate complaints and ensure compliance with privacy laws.

4. ENGAGE IN LEGAL CHALLENGES

- Support Legal Action: Encourage individuals and organizations to challenge unlawful surveillance practices through the courts. Provide resources and support for legal initiatives aimed at protecting privacy rights and holding governments accountable for overreach.

- File Freedom of Information Requests: Utilize freedom of information laws to request information about government surveillance programs and practices, which can help expose potential abuses and inform the public.

5. BUILD ALLIANCES AND COALITIONS

- Collaborate with Advocacy Groups: Partner with civil liberties organizations, privacy advocates, and technology experts to form coalitions that collectively advocate for stronger privacy protections and challenge government overreach.

- Engage with Technology Companies: Work with tech companies to promote ethical practices regarding user data and encourage them to resist government requests for data that violate privacy rights.

6. PROMOTE ALTERNATIVE TECHNOLOGIES

- Support Privacy-Enhancing Technologies: Encourage the development and use of technologies that enhance privacy, such as encrypted communication tools and decentralized data storage solutions. These technologies can help individuals maintain control over their data and reduce reliance on government-controlled systems.

- Advocate for Open Source Solutions: Promote the use of open-source software that allows users to have greater control over their data and understand how their information is handled.

7. ENGAGE IN PUBLIC DISCOURSE

- Facilitate Public Discussions: Organize public forums, debates, and discussions on the implications of government surveillance and the need for privacy protection. Engaging citizens in dialogue can foster a collective understanding of the issues at stake.

- Utilize Media Platforms: Work with journalists and media organizations to raise awareness about government surveillance practices and their impact on civil liberties. Investigative reporting can bring attention to abuses and inform public opinion.

8. PROMOTE INTERNATIONAL STANDARDS

- Advocate for Global Privacy Standards: Support the establishment of international norms and treaties that protect individuals' privacy rights in the digital age. Engaging in international advocacy can help strengthen protections against government overreach globally.

- Collaborate with International Organizations: Work with organizations such as the United Nations and regional bodies to promote human rights standards related to privacy and surveillance.

Addressing government overreach in AI tracking and surveillance requires a concerted effort from individuals, advocacy groups, and policymakers. By promoting stronger data protection laws, fostering public awareness, demanding transparency, supporting legal challenges, and building coalitions, we can work towards a future that respects individual privacy rights and holds governments accountable for their surveillance practices. Engaging in public discourse and advocating for international standards will further reinforce the importance of privacy in an increasingly digital world.

By Robert Anderson Love Wins

http://RobertAndersonLoveWins.com

www.ingramcontent.com/pod-product-compliance
Lightning Source LLC
Chambersburg PA
CBHW060202060326
40690CB00018B/4206